Justin Cotts

Thank you so
much for all your
support! We love,

[signature]

Table of Contents

Dedications

God has truly blessed me with so many talents and gifts. I want to thank my heavenly father for allowing me to go through my life experiences, both the good and the bad. Everything that I have gone through has prepared me for this journey called life. I don't know what tomorrow will bring, but I know it is part of God's master plan.

This book has been inspired by many loved ones. I want to thank my family for encouraging and supporting me as I reach out and grab my dreams. I love and appreciate each one of you:

Priscilla, Clinton, Chicovia, Terrenda, and Terence.

To my entire family, I praise God for a great family heritage. You have played a big role in helping me walk with my head held high when the inevitable life circumstances happen.

I also want to thank all my friends who have motivated me to keep writing. Thank you for your support over the years and your genuine interest in my work. Every time you lent your ears to hear one of my many works in progress, it meant so much to me.

John Donne said, "No man is an island, entire of itself…" Therefore, I am so thankful for having so many people who have allowed me to be a piece of their continent. Thank you!

Introduction

Life here on earth is one big puzzle—a puzzle that will eventually work itself out piece by piece. Everything we go through prepares us for a greater road yet traveled. All the pain, hurt and confusion that we experience from day to day, builds our character. The things we try to suppress deep inside of ourselves are the very things that have developed our current dispositions on life. I would not be who I am today if it had not been for those peers who teased me in grade school, or for my loving family who unknowingly made me feel invisible as a child. If I had not failed at a couple of things in my life or if I had not attempted the things I succeeded in, where would I be?

My prayer for this book is that it will awaken the lion in you that has been hiding because of limited courage. I pray that you will come to an understanding of how limitless God is. If God's Holy Spirit lives within you, you are limitless too. If you do not believe in God, My prayer is that you will come to know Him. Get to know this awesome God who sent his only begotten son to die for your sins, so that you may have life more abundantly.

When the storms of life come your way, focus on the bigger picture. God is preparing you for your appointed time. Don't get caught up on past circumstances that you miss the vision God is trying to show you.

~Romans 8:37~
No, in all these things we are more than conquerors through him who loved us.

When Life Happens...

What was I thinking, is the theme for my life.
Wishing I could turn back the hands of time to avoid the pain of reality,
which cuts like a knife.
I'm tossing and turning at night—dreading tomorrow—scared to face the
consequences of yesterday.
Please let this all be a dream is the prayer I pray.
In the midst of crawling out of the tunnel, into the daylight, I manage to get
dragged back in somehow.
Those in the light shout out, "Joy comes in the morning, but I want my relief
right now.
The errors I've made in my life seem to play
Over and over in my head, as if they were a movie.
And every time I try to record over my faults,
The vision gets replaced by reality.
What do you do when life happens?
How do you go on?
What do you say during the times
When life seems so unfair?
How do you stop the pain of disappointments,
Or cause the tears not to flare?
I ask myself these questions, knowing I may never know the answer.
But it gives me a chance to soak in my own mess
While depression spreads in my body like cancer.
After the pity party is over, I alone
Am left as the clean up committee.
And I don't know how to begin putting
My life back together.
Out of all the forecast, books,
And infomercials in the world
Nothing prepared me for this type of weather.
There I was planning my future
But my current circumstance was in disarray.
As more drama on top of drama piled on my plate,
It left my spirit in dismay.
"I trust you Lord," is what I wanted to scream out.
But it was so hard to do, because I wanted to know
What these trials were all about.

So I find myself asking the question again.
What do you do when life happens to you?
Well I discovered that there was not a home remedy
Or some secret class you could take.
The answer was quite simple, although very hard to grasp.
I had to finally learn from my mistakes.

<u>When life happens to you,</u>
<u>What will you do?</u>
<u>Will you call on God</u>
<u>To help you get back up on your feet</u>
<u>Or will you fall back and retreat?</u>

Don't Pass By

Looking around at the world today,
I stand convicted of the things I
Should have done, **could** have done
Would have done,
But will do tomorrow.
Today, however, I simply let pass by.
I'm reminded of the many faces I see
On a day-to-day basis, but still pass by.
Whether too content with my salvation status
Or maybe just too shy.
Either way, I still just PASS BY.
Not even to stop and just say, Hi.
How is your day or what about
Your eternity?
If not so good, have you tapped into Christ
To find out what he has called you to be?
Instead, I busily pass by.
Not willing to feed my testimony
To those souls hungry for a word
Or even break my silence
And let God's voice be heard.
Moving too quick, that I don't even
Realize that I'm being held accountable
For not sharing God's precious Gospel.
For God is calling me, a soldier in His army,
To stand up and be bold.
To not continue to pass others by,
But to stop and minister to souls
And bring them into the fold.
So in order to get others to join me on
This victorious road that God has already paved
I'm making a plea and a public service announcement,
GET SAVED!

~ Romans 10:9! ~
"If you confess with your mouth that Jesus is Lord and believe in your heart that God raised Him from the dead, you will be saved."

Tears of Joy

The one thing that I know
Is that I don't have to cry tears of sorrow.
I've been broken and kicked down,
I've been tossed and turned around.
I've experienced failure and pain
Windy storms and storms with rain.
I've endured the pressures the world has placed on me
All the harsh words and negativity.
I've wanted to give up so many times
Close the door and shut the blinds.
I've felt hopeless and afraid
And disappointed at the choices I've made.
I've wanted to give up and run
But I knew there was work to be done.
I know God has a plan for my life
Which helps me to deal with all the strife.
It helps me to look for the lesson to be learned
Instead of having pity parties of me feeling scorned.
It helps me to walk through the darkness
Without the need of feeling hopeless.
It helps me to get back up on my feet
And look at my situation as an experience and not a defeat.
So if you see a tear fall from my eye
Know that it is not tears of sadness that I cry,
But that my tears are of joy and hope.
They're tears of comfort,
Knowing God will keep me afloat.
For as long as I keep my faith in God
I can smile at the things that seem unfair and odd
And recite the one thing I know
Which is, I no longer have to cry tears of sorrow.

Addiction

Last night you appeared at my door step
And greeted me with an, "It's been so long!"
And at first, we were interacting
As if there had been nothing wrong.
Then in an instant, the peaceful moments without you were replaced with
Trips down memory lane.
Trips that caused me to keep laughing
In order to cover up the pain.
A pain that was birthed from a relationship
Of less ups and more downs
Because, back then, my addiction to your
Mess had me bound.
And I'm definitely not going to lie.
You definitely got me high.
So I would naively take a dose of your medicine
And indulge in the moment.
While my conscience sent messages to my brain marked;
STOP, PLEASE, NO, URGENT!
But I couldn't stop.
I had to continue until completion.
Then the pain I felt and the tears I cried
Made me regret my decision.
Because my spirit had warned me that
I needed to flee,
But I could not see past my own insecurities.
So I kept indulging in pleasures that were temporary
That in return left me with disappointments unnecessary.
And when it was all over, I tried to simply close the door
Hoping you would go away
For when the door is closed, the word No is so much easier to say.
But now you're back and as R. Kelly would say,
"My mind is telling me no, But my body is saying yes.
And I don't want to hurt myself,
Dealing with this same old mess,
But this test keeps coming back
Marked Redo.
Now I have to strategize, regroup and think of another method
In order to conquer you.

So this time I closed the door to consult with my counselor.
Who told me to not only confront my addiction,
But protect myself from it.
So I eagerly took everything He had to offer and
I was willing to use any protection I thought would fit.
I wrapped myself in the protection of prayer
And I got deeper in the Word
That I was able to praise God
Through each knock that I heard.
This time I was eager to answer the door
And did it without any delay.
And do you know that my old addiction fled
Before I could even fix my mouth to say hey.
And if my addiction ever returns, or another one,
I won't be hesitantly peeking through the crack,
But I'll open the door boldly and say,
God be with me now,
And God will be with me if you ever come BACK!

Saved by Jesus

I don't know much about a lot of things
I don't even know what tomorrow brings.
But I do know that when my friends
Can't seem to pick up the phone
And when I'm crying in my bed alone
God is still on the throne.
And I'm certainly not a rocket scientist
And I don't know much about biology
But I do know one certainty
Which is this simple philosophy.
If you believe in Jesus Christ
You shall be saved
And that love, joy, and peace
Takes you beyond the grave.
It even comforts you when you're
Going through so many trials
And the darkness in your journey
Seems to go on for miles.
Just knowing that God has given
His light, which shines within us
So when all else fails
It is in Him we must trust.
I'm not saying that it is going to be easy
In fact, it is a little tough
But without God in my life
Things would have been even more rough.
Not only would I have been living in
Hell on this passing phase,
But I would have to live in
Hell for my eternal days.
I would not be able to rejoice
In the Lord and receive my inheritance.
Instead I would have had to reap
The harvest of my ignorance.
And I'm definitely not saying I deserve His
Grace or mercy, for I'm far from being perfect
But If God gives me the choice of
Eternal life, I'm surely going to take it.

So for me, being wrapped up in God's
Merciful—loving arms, is where I'll continue to remain
For, "to live is Christ
And to die is to gain (Philippians 1: 21)."

Stand Up

Will the real Christians please stand up, because there is work to do?
The harvest is plentiful, but the workers are few.
I need you to be a sheep amongst wolves and not a wolf amongst sheep.
Be about your father's business through the day
And meditate on Him when you sleep.
See at first I was a full time wolf, but a sheep on the side.
I was representing the world boldly, but hiding my Spirituality inside.
I said that I was saved by the blood of Christ, but what actions did I show?
I was an anonymous Christian wanting to reap but never willing to sow.
You couldn't pick this Christian out of a line up even if I told you my name,
Because the actions of the world and mine were pretty much the same.
My motto, "The party don't start till I walk in"
Was alright with me, because I was the baddest chic with an occasional sin.
I would boast about the things that I did and didn't do,
While judging my neighbor as if God had told me too.
I was hired by God, but seemed to be working for the devil.
Instead of building the kingdom I was a kingdom rebel.
You can say I was interning for the devil and he was paying me well.
For he had a high position for me straight to hell.
At first, crossing over was something I contemplated in my mind,
Until I started looking for the benefits package that I couldn't find.
Where was my healer when I needed to be healed,
My therapist telling me I can,
My lawyer when I needed to plead my case?
I guess they're only on God's insurance plan.
And since I couldn't have my cake and eat it too,
I had to choose a side to which I was going to be faithful and true.
I had already weighed my options of which team would benefit me more,
So there I stood again knocking at God's door.
Asking Him to cleanse me and forgive me of my sins,
And to restore my life from the outside and from within.
Without hesitation, God took me in His arms and welcomed me home,
And I knew from that moment, in His arms is where I belong.
So now I'm promoting the gospel
Like a travel agent without commission.
Just wanting more souls saved with a ticket to heaven is all I'm wishing
I'm trying to recruit players to a team that is guaranteed to be victorious
But I need some help painting the picture of this eternal life

That is nothing less than glorious.
So will the real Christians please stand up, because there is work to do?
The harvest is plentiful, but the workers are few.
I need you to be a sheep amongst wolves and not a wolf amongst sheep.
Be about your father's business through the day
And meditate on Him when you sleep.

Discerning

You said it was all right
And that you understood
In fact you said if you could turn back
The hands of time and do the same, you would.
So why is it that when faced
With the simple truth
The understanding you had disappeared
Like POOF!
And now the new you is trying
To change my point of view,
Threatening that if I don't
Our relationship will be through.
Getting frustrated sexually
And telling me that it's okay to sin occasionally.
I'm not free from sin
But I'm not trying to add anymore to my list
For if I do, you are not
Going to give me the blessings I'll miss.
Remember that being with you
Was a choice that *I* made.
So don't think for one second that the
Thought of losing you has me afraid.
If you can't handle my
Gentle touch or my sweet kiss
You can feel free to leave
Without the thought to reminisce,
About our relationship
For you had your chance.
The next guy will give me genuine romance.
The next guy will share my same (or)
Similar ambitions and philosophy
And the best part is, that I won't be
Waiting on him and he won't be waiting on me.

Godly Men

Ladies, there is something
About a spiritual man,
That's too deep for most
Unbelievers to truly understand.
A man who is completely and
Sincerely dedicated to God
For it's his actions that lets
One know, he's not putting on a façade.
A man who is interested in touching
My heart and mind and not my body.
A man who calls me a woman of God
And not a typical hood-rat hottie.
A man who up-lifts me spiritually
And deposits something into my life
Who's not out to sleep with me
For I am somebody's future wife.
A man who stands strong in his faith,
Believing in something.
Instead of being in the world
Standing for nothing.
So ladies when you see this man on
The street, know that this is not your average male
Who is out in the world to conquer the
Possession of every female,
But this man has chosen to gain a new start
For he is a man after God's own heart.

True Love Waits

I'm impatient about a lot of things:
The kind of car I'll drive and the grades I'll make,
The tight clothes I'll put on and the men I'll date.
I'm just impatient!
See, I've tried this waiting around thing
Sitting, hoping that something good might come
While my friends sat in the back ground
Clowning me, saying my rationale was dumb.
I tried to be patient when my parents
Started yapping off at the mouth,
Grounding me, punishing me, scolding me,
Doing everything, but letting me out the house.
If this is what they mean by long-suffering,
I'm stretched to the capacity.
I've been waiting so long that I have
Become both bitter and angry.
I'm to the point where I refuse to sit in traffic
I refuse to stand in a line,
I refuse to stop and think
Because even that wastes time.
I am just impatient.
See I'm too impatient to stop and think about
How my actions are damaging my soul.
Or how I'm moving too fast that I'm delaying
God's will for my life to unfold.
I'm hurting those people close to me
Who are watching me race to a dead end.
An end that forces me to be still
And wait until God says when.
But because I'm so restless, I'll bump into that
Brick wall so many times, looking for a trapped door,
Until patience finally knocks me out
And lays me flat on the floor,
Forcing me to look up at my creator
Who has been patient all the while
Longing for the return of
His lost and impatient child.
And if love is patient and love is kind

It is that very same love of God to which I have been blind.
So If I claim to love the Lord,
I'll stop accepting the devil's baits
And I'll be patient with God
Because True Love Waits.

What If?

She sits in the corner wondering—how, when, where, why,
As an excessive amount of sadness and tears swell up in her eye.
She can't fathom how one day everything can be so great
And the next day everything turns into shambles.
Too ashamed to turn to anybody for help
So this situation she independently tries to handle.
When in public, she walks with her head held high
And her smiles seem to never miss a beat.
But on the inside, her spirit is dying,
Because she has been overtaken by the plague of defeat.
The people she encounter subconsciously feel her pain
Although they all ignore the severity of the issue
Because they are not willing to address her situation
Another day of her depression continues.
And without an ounce of regret
She contemplates putting an end to all of her pain.
Not realizing that this temporary life of ups and downs
Was not lived in vain.
To her there is no light at the end of the tunnel,
Instead there seems to be many more trials.
No one is there to tell her that joy will come in the morning
And that this darkness will only last for a little while.
There isn't anyone to show her how precious she is,
Or to comfort her with their related testimonies.
Everybody will have to wait and share their speech
During her final ceremony.
She sits with the phones unplugged
So no one can call to say they love her.
With a glass of water in one hand and
A bottle full of pills in the other
She utters the words
"Only God Can Save Me."
Then she proceeds to conclude the
Final chapter of her misery.
What if I would have said something?
What If I could have done something?
What if you would have opened your mouth,
Held out your hand, or done anything.

I guess now we will never know.
But the next time we perceive someone to be hurting
A seed of encouragement we will more than likely sow.

Do You Know?

Do you know?
I used to run the streets
Trying to imitate everyone I'd meet.
Do you know?
The trouble I got in
The pain, as a result, I felt within
Do you know?
That the devil was trying to win me over
Everything I did was in darkness
And I was continuously looking over my shoulder.
Do you know?
I was losing my will to fight
I was losing every thing my integrity had
Struggled to hold on to so tight.
Do you know?
That the words that came out my mouth were words
Of vulgar and words of negativity
My actions were the result of a girl who was hurting heavily.
Do you know?
The people I hung out with did not have my best intentions,
But they accepted me as long as HIS name was never mentioned.
Do you know?
That at first that was all right with me
Because I was eating the lies the devil fed me.
Do you know?
That God had a different plan in mind
For He opened my eyes to the devil's deceit
During a time when I was blind.
Do you know?
I saw a girl who was drowning in an
Unnecessary pool of sin
All because she had not let Jesus Christ in.
Do you know?
God showed me what love is and what it meant to love myself
He removed those things in my life that were damaging my health
Do you know?
That I'm not ashamed of my past and the things I've done.
I even have a new opinion of the things I consider to be fun.

Do you know?
That I don't have to be of the world to be in the world
But I can live a victorious life, for God has transformed this girl.
Do you know?
That if God can do it for me
He can do the same for you
For there is nothing that my God cannot do?
Do you know?

Beating the Odds

I've been hustling in this game call life for a while,
Trying to unlearn the fallacies about advancing,
Education and saving, that I learned as a child.
I've been busting my behind trying to maintain this
Non-advancing working class status,
While some of the wealthier citizens are sipping
On high price margaritas in their inherited palaces.
It's ironic how I'm struggling in a country
That was built by me, but not made for me
Every month it seems I'm trying to turn
Change into the money for the rent,
But still coming up missing at least one cent
So I attempt to turn ignorance into wisdom
And foolishness into knowledge.
I begin to mix my street smarts with book smarts
And successfully obtain a degree from college.
I refuse to live my life in shackles anymore.
Trapped inside of four walls of misconceptions
And too afraid to run out of the open door.
I can be liberated from the shackles that were
Placed on my mind by me
And tear down the wall of pessimism
That prohibits me from being set free.
Instead of having on-going,
Well thought about fantasies,
I can turn my dreams into realities.
Remembering that I can do all things
Through Christ that strengthens me,
I can first overcome myself and then strive to
Be more than what others thought I would be.
For if a little bit of knowledge is a powerful thing,
Then my God given wisdom can move mountains.
So instead of drinking the lies that the world feeds me
I would rather sip from God's data fountain.

Content

Surrounded by steady noise and a constant beat
The pitter-patter of rushing feet
The grinning and frowning faces
As I walk down the street.
In the midst of nature's glory,
Which tells a relaxing story
Of how everything else in the environment
Goes through life without worry.
Ironically, I find myself in the middle of a tornado.
Water is all around and the winds
Are blowing rapidly
And as I try to hold on, the ground
Is slipping from underneath me.
I'm drifting into the eye of the storm
And no one is there for me to hold on to.
In this tempest of trials, I lay drenched
And helpless with no one to pull me through.
All I want to do is cry, but the tears
Can't seem to find its way.
All my emotions are bottled up inside, ready to explode one day.
It seems as if I'm the only one lacking
That inner peace.
I've tossed all of my balls up in the air
And they have all come crashing down at one time
Causing my serenity to be buried with despair.
As I approach the eye of the storm with fear,
I am overwhelmed by its calm nature.
My problems seem to melt away
And all I can seem to do is pray.
"Lord help me to gain this inner peace everyday.
I want to be like the birds flying around a tree
Who are content throughout every season
Because they have a God that reigns for eternity."

Pursuit of Love

I've been looking for love in all the wrong places
And my pursuit of happiness has been defined by several different faces.
The emotional roller coasters of
Slow lows and fast highs
Has been defined by several different guys.
I lived by the philosophy which stated,
"You do all that you can to keep a man."
Even if that meant putting aside my morals for some temporary affection
that washed away after his erection. I would do it.
Even if that meant putting my pride aside
While I boosted up his ego while he tore mine's down
Just to get a night out on the town. I would do it.
For I wanted to be in a relationship by any means necessary.
Even if that meant my religious beliefs had to come secondary.
See these guys specialized in the sales pitches without the warning labels.
They told you all the good. While disguising the
Bad—an undercover fable.
And when the fairy tale was over and my happily ever after
Walked out the book.
I could not have imagined how much dignity they took.
And not because they robbed me of it, but because I wrapped it up in nice
little package and sent it down a secret passage that had an implied sign that
said no returns, for I got no returns on the amount of love I put out
Only lessons learned.
And I'm tired of learning the same old lessons from the same old stories.
That have me sounding like a Jamaican,
Screaming out no worries,
But on the inside I'm dying and crying out
To be loved
Not knowing that love starts from within
And comes from above.

A Dancer's Dream

I always wanted to dance as a little girl.
In fact, I dreamed it would be my dance that would inspire the world.
So I practiced day after day and hour after hour.
Tired and sweating, but practicing with aggression and power,
Because I had a dream!
I wanted to be one of the Alvin Ailey dancers
So I practiced like I stepped onto the set of Fame.
I was going to keep practicing until my opportunity came.
Feeling discouraged at times, I would sit in my room praying and crying;
Wondering why God had not acknowledged the fact that I was trying.
I was a young girl with much ambition
Begging the world to give me a chance;
To prove to the world that I could dance.
One day while dancing, I made a wrong turn into the wrong direction
But this one guy thought it was a dance of perfection.
So he approaches me about a job opportunity to
Launch his new album where he's from
And if all goes well the money and more opportunities would come.
So without hesitation I said yes, not knowing it was a test of my faith.
But the chance to dance was all I could smell
And the thought of money was all I could taste.
In an instant, my dreams of being on stage in a Broadway production
Were reduced to dancing on stage with a lot of sexual seduction.
But I still had a dream.
So I convinced myself that dancing in these late night videos
Was going to make a way.
A way that would lead to the dream gig I have been imagining each day.
After a while, I realized that the only doors being opened,
Were the cousins of the doors before.
Once I got tired of being pimped by the industry, I decided I did not want to
dance for the world any more.
So I went back to my private studio and began to dance my heart out.
I danced and danced until I had erased every ounce of every doubt.
There's no doubt that I was born to dance and not just to be another girl
known in a sex symbol role,
But known as a girl who was born with a purpose and a goal

Ready to Die

I say that you are not ready to live
Until you are ready to die.
Now, you may ask the question why,
But if God were to come back tomorrow
Or better yet today,
What closing statement during judgment time would you say?
Would you stand before the Lord claiming you
Were a good person in your lifetime?
And if you look up the word humanitarian in the dictionary,
It would be your picture He'd find.
Would you show him the highlights of your resume
Or a list of your best credentials?
Would you tell him that in high school you got voted the student
With the most potential?
Or tell him how you fed the homeless
And gave to the poor.
You managed to make it through all the pain and suffering
That you had to endure.
And if that's not impressive enough,
What else could you possibly say,
That would convince God to let you into His gates
On that particular day?
See, I'm not claiming that your actions don't reflect your heart, because faith
without works is dead.
But works can't get you into heaven alone,
Regardless of the great life you've lead.
Do you know Jesus, God's one and only begotten son,
Who died for your sins?
Have you accepted him into your life
And allowed him to transform you from within?
If you don't know Jesus Christ as your Lord and personal savior,
You don't truly know God, no matter how many times
You try to mimic His behavior.
But I'm here to bring good news that it's not too late
In order to get your non refundable ticket into heaven's gate.
Just confess Him with your mouth, believe Him in your heart
And Jesus will enter into your life and give you a brand new start.
I don't know about you, but that's the phrase that pays

That I'm willing to say,
For I want to hear God say, "Well done thy good and faithful servant"
On judgment day.
For it is my analysis that you are not ready to live until you are ready to die.
For if God says depart from me, I never knew you, don't ask WHY!

Super Hero

Stronger than Strong
Faster than fast
He's my super Hero
Saving souls in a flash.
Better than a man a man who can leap
Over tall buildings in a single bound.
He can deliver souls that were
Lost and now found.
He's more than a muscle, bulging man who can save me from a falling tree,
He is a supernatural God who can save me for eternity.
Even in this world full of hell and sin,
God has no kryptonite.
Remember, he created the moon and the sun
Which gives us light,
So no darkness can overcome him
And claim to be greater,
For he will forever remain the head honcho in charge
With the devil as his hater.
He doesn't have to rob from the rich and give to the poor
He can pour you out a blessing through an open window or door.
More than just a savior, He is a comforter too.
So when you're feeling troubled
God's Holy Spirit that lives within, will speak life to you.
My God is so tight that He doesn't need a side kick
Nor does He need a punch line or fancy outfit.
He makes it to the scene before you think to call
And He will pick you up when you fall.
He is more than just incredible,
He is unforgettable.
He's more powerful than an egotistical wiz
Chilling at the end of a yellow brick road.
Instead of giving him some ruby slippers,
Give him your burdens and watch him lift that load
His infinite wisdom is not always understood by men, but I trust him.
He cleansed me of my imperfections by adding them to his perfections,
So I love him
I don't have to hope that he comes
He's always right on time.

I don't have to dedicate this poem to Him
Because He is the Rhyme.
He is Stronger than strong,
Faster than fast,
He's my super hero
Saving souls in a flash.

Baton

The best gift anyone could ever give her is the gift of prayer
Because prayer can change situations in her life even when she's unaware.
All she knows is that she was a given a baton and told to run,
No one told her it was tainted, filthy
And had no evidence of the father, spirit, or the son.
See forget what you heard about papa, mamma was a Rolling Stone
In fact, she did a couple of tricks and a man
Gave her everything she ever owned
And all the while, baby girl was listening; watching her momma teacher her
lessons she didn't verbally have to say.
She learned that a man is only good for a couple of things—one being his
paycheck—and it's okay if he doesn't stick around the next day.
So when she got older she became a mirror image of her mother—
An image her mother hated to see.
Although she desired more for her life, being promiscuous
Was the only way she knew how to be
Some men treated her like a used car—good for a few rides,
But eventually she'll have to be traded in.
And she was okay with that, because she had gotten use to the trend.
Her value had depreciated and so had her self worth.
Her virtue faded away a long time ago and one might even say
That her life was cursed since birth.
She has given into a generational curse that recycles low self esteem
A curse that has her dependent on other people
Instead of allowing her to dream.
She was a diamond in the rough,
Had been through so much and her life, that it made her appear to be tough.
She was emotionally beat, pimped slapped by defeat
And although she tried, she couldn't get back on her feet.
But on the outside she was a five feet, eight inch, dime piece.
Outer beauty stunning, but on the inside, so much drama to release.
Most men are mesmerized by the package she comes in,
Meaning, her physical glory,
As long as when they give her money, she gives it up,
They don't care about her true-life story.
So in return she hid her conscience behind
A hedge of denial that she had built.
This way she could hide form all her negative feelings

And never confront her guilt.
But just like David with his sling shot, this giant will fall to the ground
And all of her walls of insecurities will come tumbling down.
All it takes is for some one to hear her silent cry
And pray for her area of weakness.
Eventually the seed that was planted and watered
In her spirit will sprout awareness.
An awareness of how much God loves her and desires to dwell within.
He desires to be her source for strength and her anecdote to her sin.
She needs to know that God is a forgiving God
Who can make her whole again.
She doesn't need to be written off as a lost cause
And thrown back into a world of sin.
Prayer is the best gift anyone can ever give her
For it can change situations in her life even when she's unaware.
All she knows is that she was given a baton and told to run.
No one ever told her it was tainted, filthy and had no evidence
Of the Father, Spirit or Son.

Over The Rainbow

This soul of mine can't stay trapped in this old body forever.
So when forever comes, I imagine my spirit taking flight
In order to inherit its treasure.
But not some treasure that can be found here on Earth,
But way up high in a land far, far away,
In a land where I will see my creator face to face one day.
And there I will sing his praises of how good He's been.
I will forget about the past and rejoice in the fact
That now eternity with Him begins.
There will be no more pain, no more hurt, no more sorrow.
Everlasting joy will be available right then, right there, and tomorrow.
See I'm dreaming of a place where I will find great peace.
I've searched high and low and as far as the west is from the east,
But each time I've come up empty handed or
Recovering from a temporary fix.
And the older I get the world beats me with
Drama disguised as birthday licks.
When I turn to my left, I see diseases taking my people out in packs.
To my right, homeless people are starving and
All I can do is offer them snacks.
I work hard everyday trying to keep a job that's on standby
Scared to spend my money on steak and potatoes, so I continue to eat rye.
My family is feuding over things I can't explain
While I'm trapped in the middle, fighting back tears, trying to maintain.
And the only thing I have to hold on to is God's promise
That trouble don't Last always
Even though life hasn't been no crystal stair,
There has been and will be some good days.
Somewhere out there is a land where wars come to an end
And health care isn't a concern.
Everyone's home is a mansion and riches are given and not earned.
There's a land where unconditional love is present and overflowing.
God is there waiting for you to reap paradise
For the many seeds you have been sowing.
Somewhere over the rainbow is where I long to be,
When my journey here is complete.
After I've done all that God has required of me and I fall into a deep sleep.
I want to wake up where my troubles melt away like lemon drops.

Faith is united with truth and corruption stops.
Will you let your faith travel with me to a land abundant
With milk and honey?
Fly with me to blue skies—where there are no more rainy days,
Only days that are sunny.
When it's time to fly away, I want to enter a Never, Never Land
Full of light and no dark.
But until my rainbow comes, I'll continue to escape to heaven in my heart.

Seven Deadly Sins

I stand before you as one guilty of doing wrong.
Guilty of not being obedient to the one in which I belong.
God I'm asking you to forgive me of the past
And present sins I've committed.
Lord I'm seeking deliverance from my flesh,
So I'm not afraid to admit it.
There are so many things on my mind that I need to release.
I'm confessing my seven deadly sins in order to gain peace
Forgive me for taking credit for what I thought was my own abilities
While leaving the appreciation of your grace denied?
Forgive me for I did not know that in my vanity
I was committing the sin of pride.
Lord I've longed to have the lifestyle of someone else,
Or at least to have their amount of money.
So I need to be forgiven for the sin call envy.
Several meals I have eaten more than my eyes can see,
Therefore, placing me in the category of gluttony.
Forgive me for allowing my need to please the flesh,
Keep me from focusing on your will.
Instead of running towards you, I was tumbling down a lustful hill.
Many times my anger and frustration
has lead me down the wrong path
Journeying to destruction on a street called wrath.
And countless times I've considered the desire
For material wealth or gain as a need.
Placing me in the category of greed.
I have let sloth sneak in and become my downfall
And because of procrastination, I have yet to accept my call.
God I'm asking for forgiveness. God I need to release
The guilt of these seven deadly sins in order to gain peace.

Now or Never

I don't know how much longer I have with you
So I'm going to pour into you all I can while I can.
I'm not going to believe the hype about living forever
Because tomorrow isn't promised to any man.
I'm going to cut myself and allow my inner thoughts to
Bleed out into the open and stain the atmosphere.
I don't know what you thought you came to witness,
But this isn't your typical poet right here.
For far to long my vocal cords have been silent,
Suppressing the very thing that gives my lungs oxygen to breath.
So Allow me to testify about the goodness of God and
Give witness to the reason I believe.
If it had not been for God on my side I cannot imagine how lost I'd be.
I'd probably be in a sinful place, drowning in my own repercussions.
I would still be in the mindset to satisfy my flesh in any way possible
Whether it is acting on my lustful thoughts
Or engaging in undignified discussions.
I struggled up the mountain ready to rejoice at my own endurance,
Only to look ahead at the many more mountains I had to face.
So I called on the name of Jesus, and he carried me on the wings of eagles
Into His safe resting place.
So sharing my faith is the least I can do to show my appreciation
God has given me so many chances to get my life right.
He has given me grace and shown me mercy that I dare not
Hold back the very knowledge that can give the blind sight.
Therefore, forgive me for shouting to loud, clapping or stomping my feet.
Forgive me for sharing the gospel or getting up to do my praise dance,
But the Lord has been too good to me that
I'm going to praise him every time I get a chance.
For I don't know how much longer I have with you
So I'm going to live my life as if Jesus is coming back today.
And if you want to join me on this awesome journey,
Jump aboard and ride with me and let God lead our way.

Princess

She was a princess with the most contagious smile.
Daddy's little girl and momma's precious child.
She had the dream childhood that most people can only wish
For their future offspring
A child friendly neighborhood and a house fit for a king.
There was no drama in her life that a piece of cake couldn't repair
Life was good to her for she walked around on clouds free of care.
Walking to the beat of her own drum because she had her on style
She was daddy's little girl and mamma's precious child.
She was just a little girl trying to live out her childhood.
Trying to play in the playground of her neighborhood.
And he was just a lion on the prowl—hunting for his next prey
Plotting to steal her innocence instead of continuing to let her play.
He took her virtue from her and left it in the park.
He left her bleeding and crying out for help in the dark.
Where was mamma to comfort her and her daddy for protection?
Cake just won't do it this time and she doesn't want affection.
She wants someone to turn back the hands on the clock
The moment before the hour went tick-tock
Ten minutes before she saw that all her friends had gone
Five minutes before she should have headed home
Right before her grabbed her by her hair and pulled her amongst the trees
Kicking and screaming—yelling out please.
But there is no time machine to correct the past
There are only memories that replay over and over that will forever last
Now this princess doesn't smile anymore.
She now walks around with her head facing the floor.
Daddy's loosing control to a bottle of alcohol,
Trying to drown out the voices he wished he'd heard
When his daughter did call.
Momma's eyes are filled with rage and her faith is fading.
Their princess was in need of being rescued while they were at home waiting.
Now they're waiting on justice that their princess can't comprehend.
She needs a peace the flows like a river that only God can send.
But right now God just seems so far away
She's looking back for restoration that she feels, should have occurred the
other day.
She looked back so much that she forgot she had a future.

She forgot she had a today and tomorrow to endure.
Why did this have to happen to her—not that she wished it for someone else
But she darn sure didn't wish it for herself.
She has questions for God that she may never get the answers to.
Like why was it this trial that he allowed her to go through?
However, the God of all grace wants to restore her and make her stronger.
He wants to transform her sufferings into a testimony
She won't be ashamed of any longer.
While the devil meant to harm her, God wants to console her.
He wants to rock her in His arms and carry her on his shoulders.
And for that daddy and momma who is seeking revenge to end their anguish.
The bible says that if people plant evil and trouble,
That's what they'll harvest.
As God deals with the evildoers, pray that they continue planting seeds of love
into their child.
For the more they show their princess the love of God,
She will eventually begin to smile.

My Daddy

When the topic of dead-beat dads arise,
Fortunately I can't relate
Because my dad chose not to participate
In the sad epidemic that seems to
Be plaguing the world.
An epidemic that would have left me
As an unfortunate, fatherless girl.
So I stand up and give my dad his accolades as a father who has been there
when I was up and when I was down.
He did not just charge me off to the game as unclaimed baggage, as a result
from a careless night out on the town
He chose to plant seeds of good character
Into his children and watch them bloom
Even when weeds would grow due to the world's fertilization, he would take
the time to prune.
Through my father's actions, he showed me the true meaning of what a man
should be.
He showed me that no other man could ever love me as much as he,
But they better darn sure do their best and try!
They better do everything in their power to become the apple of my eye.
See these high standards I have for myself were set by my dad.
For he did everything he could to provide for his family
And he gave all he had.
And I appreciate my father for just being himself
For he wasn't the CEO of some big company, but he used his talents to
Create his wealth.
And if that didn't cut the check, he went out and got other jobs
To pay the bills
And still had time to say I love you, give me hugs and show me how
Unconditional love feels.
So when you talk about those low down, trifling brothers who make babies
And head out the door,
Don't mention my dad's name, for he was always present—loving his
Children down to the core.
I'm not saying my dad is perfect, but he's the best man he knows how to be.
No matter what I do and where I go I know he'll always be there for me.
So this poem is a poem of gratitude to tell you of a Job well done.
This poem is a plea that other men will follow in your footsteps,

Especially your son.
This poem will serve as an example to all the women who have given up on good black men,
Hopefully they will see the character of what a good man and father should be and find hope again.
I'm so blessed to have been your youngest daughter, your precious baby.
Thank you for being my Father and not just my Daddy!

Teacher Appreciation

This is an official shout out to all my educators out there in the world
Who have spent their careers changing the life of some little boy
Or some little girl.
You encourage one to reach their fullest potential in anyway they desire.
You are one of God's tools sent here to not only educate but to inspire.
Because of you, someone succeeded when they were expected to fail.
That class clown made it beyond college, and bypassed jail.
You are the secular version of, *Never Would Have Made It*,
For some little child.
You are the voice that tells girls they can do more than be on the video,
Girls Gone Wild.
You are the encouraging words a child may only hear during the school day.
You are the guiding force that keeps some children from going astray.
It is your dedication that directs children to the right path.
You not only motivate the students, but you motivate the staff.
Incredible is what comes to mind, when I think of how much you multi task.
Regardless of personal issues, you manage to put on your professional mask.
Educating is definitely a challenging job that you manage to do so well.
It seems you have a secret success potion
And the students are under your spell.
Disrespect and disobedience is definitely not tolerated in your presence
And without saying a word, one look is all that is needed
To demonstrate your guidance.
You are nurturing to the heart, but challenging to the mind.
You are that willing, humble spirit that is so hard to find.
It is amazing how you manage to meet children where they are.
Then you equip them with the necessary tools of life
That will carry them so far.
It is not by coincidence that you were chosen for this field.
No matter how many times people say, "You're just doing this to pay a bill."
You are patient and unselfish, when most people can't be.
You are creating future doctors and lawyers that, right now, people can't see.
And although you are unappreciated at times and highly underpaid,
You are the reason some little child walks into their potential
Without being afraid.
Your profession affects children in the present
As well as when they get older,
For they see, in addition to providing wisdom and exposure,

You provided your shoulder.
There aren't enough words to thank you for all that you do.
So, for now, please accept this simple shout-out, dedicated to you.

.

Color of Beauty

When I look into the mirror, I see the color of beauty.
I see a color imprinted by the strength of a powerful history.
Who I am lies deeper than just the surface appearance.
For I am the reflection of my ancestors' endurance.
I am over two hundred years of slavery
Wrapped up into a 20th century baby.
I am the product of hopes and wishes of freed slaves who weren't really free.
I am the walking dream that Martin always envisioned his people would be.
The way I climb up the ladder of success, proves that I'm Free at Last.
I am every negro spiritual song come to past
The way I walk with my head held high, represents victory.
The way I speak eloquently and dress for success, spells dignity.
You can tell that there is a since of pride about myself
Now that I have stop eating the lies that were fed to me,
Which degraded my self wealth.
I am every African American girl who was denied
The gift of learning to read.
I am every salve, whose master thought he was just raising
Another cotton, picking breed.
Underneath my business suit of success, lie wounds
Deeper than the eyes can see.
But those cuts now have scars that represent healing
And the birth of a strong testimony.
The word "Overcome" is my middle name,
So when I think about my past I dare not feel ashamed.
I'm running the race that great men and women have set up for me.
A race for freedom, integrity and equality.
I'm running this race for people like Sojourner Truth, Fredrick Douglas,
W.E.B Dubois, Mary Mcloude Bethune, El Hajj Malik El Shabazz and
Martin Luther King Jr. and I'm running with dedication.
See I'm not merely running this race for the past, but I'm running for the
present and the up coming generation.
I'm running this race so when people ask my future children who they are;
It will be plan to see,
That they are the beneficiaries of a strong, beautiful and powerful
Black History

In Love

I love you! I love you! I love you!
God I just needed to say those words to you,
Because I am in love with you.
I love you because you first loved me
I love you because you offered me salvation at the price marked Free.
I love you because when I was drowning
In my own mess,
You still being God, did not love me any less.
I love you at night, when I'm sleep and when I rise,
I love you because I'm foolish and you're wise.
I love you because you do not hold that against me, especially when
sometimes, the opposite of Christ-like is my identity.
See I love you more than minorities love Obama.
I love you more than babies love their mama.
More than sunshine on a three day weekend
More than teens love some new J's or a hip-hop trend.
I am insanely spinning out of control,
Losing my mind and don't know what to do,
Amazed, astonished, head over heels,
Completely and totally in love with you.
You inspire me like nature to a painter,
A rhythmical beat to a dancer
MLK Jr. to a hopeful generation
The ideal of change to a distraught nation.
I am in love with you
Because you are the real deal.
In those moments when I thought I was fighting my own wars, I discovered
it was you on the battle field.
You have been the light piercing through the dark places. My first and
second wind when I'm running life's races.

The Essence of Lu

When wondering where the secret
Of LuVenia White lies,
The answer is simple,
It lies within my eyes.
See my eyes are the windows into my soul
And the more you look
The true character of me will unfold.
Giving one a peek into my body's
Most prized possession.
And for all who dare
To look, the view is a guaranteed blessing.
Once you get past my hard core exterior
You'll find a protected soft, sweet and sensitive interior.
There will lay a girl with a lot of
Heart and a lot of charm
A shy girl that just longs to be in someone's arms.
A girl who thinks that love is so far away
And even if it's close
Its direction is pointing in the opposite way.
You'll find a girl who wants to
Do the things in life that are right
And to get what she wants
She is willing to put up the fight.
A girl will be discovered who has a little bit
Of style and a little bit of grace.
A girl who even has a ghetto side
That is sometimes hard to embrace.
Still being captivated by the true inner me,
You'll find a girl who is straight up
Down to earth
And who has been that way
Since the time of her birth.
The more you look the more you'll see
That I'm still very mysterious
And that mystery might appear
To be quite dangerous
For there are qualities about me
That can't quite be defined

Because my character is truly one of a kind.
So if you dare to come into my life
You better think not once, but twice
For what you see is definitely
Not all that you get,
Because I'm an original wonder
You will never forget.

Waiting

I feel it near me, I can smell it
Around the corner, taste it in the atmosphere,
But the harsh reality is; if it is
Not in my face it is not really here.
I have heard rumors about it
And many grand stories
I've heard of the joy of those
Who've experienced it in all of its glory.
Its mysterious nature
Somehow appeals to me,
Drawing me closer that
One day I'll be able to see;
The same picture that has
Managed to capture so many people
And have them running
Merrily to the steeple.
I'm longing for the day when I can stand
Up proud and say, "I'm in the majority,"
And no longer standing
Amongst the lonely rejected minority.
I'm even looking forward to the gloomy
Nights and misty weather,
For knowing I want be alone
Makes the situation better.
My bitter being longs to
Be sweetened by its gentle kiss,
Filled with its secret of romance
And unimaginable bliss.
You've denied yourself from me for so very long
That the first time I receive
You I don't want it to be wrong.
I want to make myself readily available
For that gift that comes from above
That wonderful gift that
Is none other than true LOVE!

My Version

I saw you standing over there
And I wanted to know your name.
So I did my shake and move
And got you to follow into my game.
However still being a lady
I could not complete the task
So I waited to see if you had a plan
Then I let your creativity unmask.
See the slight eye contact we made
Was all apart of my scheme.
For I did not want to find out
How appearing to bold would seem.
I abided by the old fashion rule
Of letting a man be a man
For my mama always told me
To let the male seek out your hand.
Slowly attracting you like a magnet,
Hypnotizing you with my best features
Captivating you with my luxurious smile
Which appeals to most seekers.
I was delighted that you picked up my
Intense vibe and welcomed it in.
I made myself readily available so you'd
Know this challenge you would win.
When you approached, I played the shy
Card and I did play it well,
For I could tell you had no idea that you
Had just been caught up in my sly little spell.
Nevertheless, I'll let you tell the story
The way you choose to let it unfold.
But, between me and you, let me tell it
And this is the truth being told.

Not For Sale

Roses are red and violets are blue,
You're thinking, I've heard poems like this,
But wait a minute, because I'm not through.
See, those were the same red roses
You were leaving at my door,
And the same blue violets
You kept going to the store and ordering more
Thinking that's all it took.
That you could give me a kiss on my cheek
And you thought you'd have me shook.
While I continuously got hurt
And you watched the pain and anger grow
Deeper and deeper,
Yet told your homeboys,
I'll just buy her something and I'll be able to keep her.
Now how lame was that
That you thought I'd forever be in your trap
Of flowers, candies, roses, dinners and a movie
While you set up there and mentally, NOT physically,
But verbally abused me.
Well check it; your chances and strikes
Are out the window
And all the mess you put me through,
Please believe, you can take that to the next door.
Because I'm tired of being fake,
And I'm tired of being polite.
I'm tired of receiving your apologetic phone-
Calls late at night.
I'm tired of kissing on a man
Who doesn't quite understand
That our relationship is never going to be right,
For just like our relationship
Along with me being naïve,
That has sunken and a new me has taken flight
Who is no longer looking for a part-time lover,
Or a man who is going to be with me only undercover.
A man who steady makes excuses
And apologizing, while at the same time lying,

Which by the way, I was never buying.
So the next time you think about the things that
I want, or even the things that I like,
Just remember this tiny tad bit,
I'm going to tell you and your junk
To go take a HIKE.
Cause just like your roses are red and your violets,
That made me feel so blue,
Believe me, the relationship you think
You have with me is good and through.

Conditional Love

He said he loved me
And I honestly believed that he did.
But it hit me that his rationale
On love, were the same views of a kid.
There I stood, a young woman
Who had fallen in love with a young boy
Whom did not understand what I needed or
Wanted and therefore treated me like a toy.
This man used and abused me
Until he got bored,
Then put me on the shelf,
Subconsciously unplugging
Our relationship as if it were a cord.
Loving me was not as easy
As saying I do or saying yes.
For when graded on his actions of love
Well, let's just say he failed that test.
He couldn't even cheat his way though it
Or even pretend that he knew it
Matter of fact, he just threw his cards
On the table and ran like fluid.
Never looking back to say
I'm sorry for causing you to shed so many tears
Or to stand apologetic for
Having me waste so many of my years.
He must not have read the fine print on
The relationship, which said:
May endure hardships or stormy weather.
Instead, it appeared "sunny days," is all he read.
And maybe he can go on
And live his life to the fullest
And never think back to the one
Girl he lost who was the truest,
The one who would have forever and
Continuously had his back.
And the quality of patience I possess
Other girls might surly lack
A girl who thought, love could be obtained by

Ignoring his behavior in hopes
That it would go away,
Instead of focusing on how his love
For me varied from day to day.
The problem is, I fell in love with an idea of how I thought
A man should love me
Instead of falling in love with
A man who did love me and did it unconditionally.

Unconditional love

God, it's funny how the love I've been missing
Has been in front of my face the whole time.
I've been pushing you aside in order
To fine unconditional love in mankind.
I packed my bags and walked out of your safety,
Into the arms of another man.
And when his love wasn't sufficient enough
It left me with questions I couldn't understand.
I thought I was unappealing and worthless,
Because I allowed each man to take the best of me.
I poured all I could into a bottomless container
That drained me to the point of being empty.
At the end of the day
I had nothing to give back to you, my creator.
Nothing but mundane prayers and counterfeit promises, to get back into my
word later.
I became that, praise you only on sunny days, kind of chic
But would flee when bad weather appeared
Or when you started to discipline me with reality licks.
I put your love on the shelf,
So that I could play with the world
While the world cheated on me
And made me feel like everything, but a pearl.
Mr. Cellophane is probably what you've
Been screaming out to me as I walk by.
I've been looking right through you
As you try to catch my eye.
What a hypocrite I've been for throwing stones
At a man for loving me the same way that I have been loving you.
When my love was put to the test, it turned out
That I was the one who was unfaithful and untrue.
God I thank you for being patient and
For never giving up on me.
Most of all, I thank you for loving me
UNCONDITIONALLY!

Who Are You?

Mr. Thief in the night, could you please reveal yourself to me?
I'm tired of being robbed by a stranger whose identity I can see.
I've been dating a man of many faces
And I have still yet to see the true you.
So I'm asking you to help me solve this mystery
By giving me one last and final clue.
Might you be my night and shinning armor, who comes in on his white
horse
And saves me from destruction, to place me on the right course.
Or are you the milk man who sneaks in the back door
Leaving no traces of the night before.
Could you be my broker, causing my interest to rise,
Or could you be a bill collector, just one depressing surprise?
Maybe I thought you were a lawyer
And that this was just one simple relationship case you could handle.
But then again you could have been the president,
Because our relationship turned out to be one big scandal.
You must have been MJ
Because everybody wanted to get with, I mean be like Mike.
You must have played in the movie Life
Because you just couldn't get right.
I believe you did a little boxing, because you knocked me off my feet.
Every time you touched me, you made me weak.
So you must have been Mohamed Ali,
Because you had me floating like a butterfly
And then you stung me like a bee.
Maybe you were a placebo for love
And I was a hypochondriac,
Because I had fooled myself into believing I needed your bull crap.
Then again, what if you were just an ordinary guy
Who just was not meant for me.
And the delusion of other faces was the picture I wanted to see.
In an attempt to fall in love, I fell without caution
So I blamed you for the heartache,
In hopes that the fall would be softened.
When in reality, you was no good when I meet you
And you stayed consistent all the while.
Writing this poem is just the final stage of my denial.

Dedication

Some people said leave,
He's not for you.
But somehow I believed that
I could make this man be true.
I said it was dedication
That brought us through,
But it was dedication that
Simply left me feeling blue.
They said, "girl, why do you let this man
Make you sad, make you mad, make you cry?"
Well, because of the time I'd invested,
What was I suppose to do; say good-bye?
I said it was my dedication
That kept me around
But in actuality it was my dedication
That had me bound.
They said there were signs saying
The relationship was wrong as big as day,
But like a fool, because of dedication
I decided to stay.
Thinking I could change things
And somehow make them right,
Not realizing that sometimes
You loose the fight.
But I said it was my dedication,
Thinking you was good for my health.
And it was dedication
That had me playing myself.
They said I was num to the pain
And I did not need to be subjected to it any more.
Which was funny because,
The last time you hurt me,
It was like déjà vu, because you had hurt me before
But I said, it was my dedication
That could change you from a boy to a man
And now it's that exact
Dedication that I can no longer stand.

So whatever our relationship
Was about or even for,
It is over, for now I am
Dedicated to walking out the door.

Hard-headed

Something told me NO!
But knowing me, I had to test the water.
I was only planning to find out a little bit about
Your character, but I tripped and fell over the boarder.
Your bad boy persona was
Drawing me closer like a magnet
Causing my curiosity to grow stronger
Setting my conscience at a panic.
I was arguing with myself
Saying should I or should I not
But the answer to the question was
I had already been got.
Feeling bold, I got up the nerve to approach you
And was flattered when you accepted my advance
However, still a bit disturbed
As to why I'd wanted to take a chance.
I mean, your rap sheet was far from
What I would consider to be good
But here I stood waiting patiently in line
Hoping that there would be something different
About you, that I would find.
Willing to put aside reality
And lean on the 'maybe' factor.
"Maybe once you're with me
I'll be able to change your character."
Naively fooling myself on so many different levels
While burying my dignity deeply with a shovel.
And then, like a strong force
Tugging at my heart, I was caught up.
Shoot; I was yearning for your presence
Over dosing in your essence
I was messed up.
All because I wanted a guy with
A little bit of edge to enter into my life
To stir up this good girl mixture
With your bad boy spice.
And when the measure of what

You mixed was more than I could bare
I found myself trying to gather up the little
Bit of integrity I had left to spare.
In order to rescue a compromising girl,
Who had lost touch with reality
But was now willing to move on
And let go of her bad boy fantasy.

The Power of a Kiss

A kiss so soft
A kiss so sweet
A kiss so gentle
A kiss so deep
Captivating my mind
And captivating my thoughts
This kiss erasing all of
My fears and all of my doubts
Putting me in complete
Isolation with this guy
Taking me on a natural
And unimaginable high
Making me question
The next move to take
And having me wonder
The next move he'll make
Body is trying to
Resist temptation
While were speaking in tongue
An understood conversation
The passion of this kiss
Sending chills up my spine
Pulling me into new dimensions
Of a world so divine
My body melts with
Each touch of his lips,
As we hold each other closer
With his hand upon my hips
The look in his eyes
Stimulating pure desire
Of intensified heat
Hotter than fire.
He's got my toes curling
And he got my body swirling
He's got me seeing
Fireworks in the daytime
I'm talking about bright lights and colors

Of every kind.
The power of this kiss
Is so intense,
That it is almost
Hypnotic in a sense.

Burn

You came into my life like an unpredicted breeze
And for a moment you set my heart at an ease.
I was appearing to be young, but truly not naïve
Yet everything you told me, I was tempted to believe.
You had my eyes wide open,
I was an impressionable youth
Who thought I had all the answers and could distinguish the truth.
I knew exactly what I wanted
And you fed me all the right lines
You had me so blinded by infatuation
That I completely ignored all the negative signs.
You had me feeling like a child standing outside of a free candy store;
Feeling all sensitive, soft and tender.
And everybody who knows me
Knows that is far outside of my character.
I completely stepped outside of myself
In order to be with you.
Only to find out that you were not really true.
You were the epitome of what they call a ladies' man—
One who says all the right things
To get all that they can.
Your words were empty
Therefore, leaving my love in vain.
For it was apparent that the way I felt about you
You did not feel the same.
I was just another girl to add to your list of statistics
Who thought your feelings were legit
And that your words were realistic.
I was tricked and fooled by a guy
So suave and debonair
That I allowed you to walk out of my life
Leaving me broken hearted
As if you did not even care.
Not only broken hearted,
But left with a little bit of shame
The shame of a bruised ego
That was overtaken by game.

But I refuse to get upset,
For there was a lesson to be learned,
Which is, I'll get over it and I'll grow stronger,
But this time I'll just have to let it burn.

Good Enough

The relationship we have is good
And it has lasted longer than I thought it would.
I'm attracted to you and hopefully you to me
And we even sometimes form a unique chemistry.
The relationship is good...enough
You even meet some of the qualities
That I'm looking for in a man.
You even have some of those negative
Qualities that I can't stand.
And realizing that I'm not perfect
I know you've dealt with a lot of my flaws
And sometimes dealing with my negativity
Has probably brought your feelings
for me as well to a pause,
We're each other's good...enough
But maybe I should just be overjoyed
With a love that is simply O.K.
A love good enough that other girls
Might usually even prefer to stay.
Maybe I shouldn't wonder what else
Is out there for me
And just devote my time to
Pretending that I'm actually happy.
I should just stay and settle for this good enough
But my thoughts are communicating
Too much with my heart
And my heart is telling me that
We need to be set apart
Apart from this delusion that
What's right is definitely wrong
And that to each other our hearts do not belong.
No more staying and settling for good enough
To be honest, our relationship is bland
And not in the least ecstatic.
I'm looking for something a little less
Mediocre and a tad bit more dramatic.
I'm not looking to be content

I'm looking for nothing but the best
And this relationship has really
Put my desires to the test.
I want a guy who complements me
In all of my ways
One whom I can be with for the rest of my days.
One who prays with me and allows God to be the head of his life.
I want a man that I can see myself in the future becoming his wife.
So leaving this relationship might
Appear to be really tough,
But to be real, I can't stay
And settle for simply good enough.

Heart Speaks

My life has never been an open book
But page by page I'll allow you to
Take an exclusive look.
You're different from most of the guys
That I have come to know,
For when you speak, the purpose
Is not to put on a show.
You came at me with an approach
That was so sincere,
That being with you was an option
I did not fear.
Without feeding my ego, you made
Me feel like I was floating on cloud nine,
By encouraging my true personality to shine.
You promoted qualities in me
That I could not presently see
And through my ups and my downs
You prayed for me consistently.
You complemented my character
Instead of dominating over it.
By allowing me to be my own complete person,
I began to love you for it.
I began to break down the wall
Of protection guarding my heart
And let you massage each
And every broken part.
I slowly dealt with my commitment issues
And trusted you to not let me down.
For when I was looking to be disappointed
Satisfaction is all I found.
I'm not sure where this will lead us
But the fact is, I'm willing to go,
For I now understand that it is O.K. to listen to
My heart saying yes, even when my mind says no.

Crazy

It's crazy how you've got me
As if someone has shot me
With a love bullet of intensity
Piercing through my body with much velocity.
It's crazy how the thought of you has me amazed
And one glimpse of you can send me into an unrecoverable daze.
It's crazy how I'm captivated by your mere essence
And how when you're not around me, I'm
Longing to be in your presence.
It's crazy how I'm mesmerized
Every time I look into your deep brown eyes
And how when you're around me, that's when
My body temperature slowly begins to rise.
It's crazy how I feel like I'm in an
Obstacle or roller coaster;
Going over emotional speed bumps
And doing high jumps
To compete in a race for your affection
While it appears that other girls
Are also longing for your deep chocolate complexion.
It's crazy how we have not even touched
And we have not even kissed,
But us in the future appears to be pure bliss.
It's crazy how a crush can last so long
And build up over time
To become so strong
And how us in the future,
Not being together, battling every trial
And sticking out every weather
Is just plan crazy.

Liberation

What's real is that I'm free to be me
I'm free to be myself
And I no longer need a man to
Define my self-wealth (repeat).
I use to wait in the shallow
Waters, awaiting your hand
Thinking I needed you to lead me into
The deep, where I could not stand.
Never willing to jump in
Without a sturdy raff
Or to travel alone
Down my own life's journey or path.
You were my security in
The mist of my insecure ways.
And that mentality caused my destination
Of empowerment to experience some slight delays.
When alone, I was a stranger to my own being.
A stranger for all the wrong reasons.
I had isolated myself, from myself
For so many wasted seasons.
And now that you're gone
And I was left here all alone
I had to turn to this stranger
To find the strength to be strong.
And now that my eyes are open
I am disgusted at the image I see.
For here lies a girl who is confused
And who is begging to be set free.
Released from the bondage of pointless relationships
That leads to a foreseeable dead end.
An end that leads to a broken heart
Left for another man to mend.
An incomplete girl, trying
To find and form complete relationships
That would put an end to all my
Depressions, flaws, and hardships.
But now, I'm sick and tired of being

Sick and tired of the same old mess,
Of coming in not even 50% of a whole person
And leaving out the relationship even less.
So after taken a private retreat
To fall in love with myself
God helped me discover that I
No longer need a man to define my self-wealth.

You Want What You Can't Have

They say you always want what you
Can't have and I found that to be true
For I knew that I could not
Completely have all of you
But I was willing to stick
Around and fake it
And pretend that we could make it.
In my mind I was convinced
That you were just taking it slow.
However, the fact that you did not want to
Commit to one person was the reality I didn't know.
I was blinded by your controversial
Words and actions
That had me believing I was your point guard
And at the end of the day you would
Be standing outside, in front of my yard.
But it was revealed to me that I was just
Riding the bench and waiting my turn,
While you gave others playtime; and the longer I
Didn't know the more points I'd earn.
Many other good teams were recruiting
But I stayed faithful and true.
I was a loyal player getting played by you.
Sometimes it takes an injury to
Get one out of the game
So when my heart got broken I had
No one but myself to blame.
I was like a dog chasing after its own tail;
You were not trying to be caught.
And after running around in circles and
Getting dizzy, I finally saw my fault.
So as I finally try to retire from this mess,
Here you come knocking at my door
Claiming I'm the one that your heart longs for.
Well, be that as it may
But the message of, "you always want what you can't have,"
Is the lesson you will learn today.

My Bad

I'm sorry; I did not mean to offend you.
But then again, I did not mean to captivate you either.
So whose fault is it really?
Yours, mine, or neither.
See there I was minding my business
In my own little space,
When you decided to approach me
Like some little cat to be chased.
Coming on strong with some weak lines.
Like, "shawdy, I'm about to make you mine."
Somebody please do me a favor
And point out the appeal.
How about trying it again,
And next time attempt to keep it real.
Try making me laugh or starting
Up a casual conversation.
Instead of bum rushing me for my number,
Like you don't have patients.
Try introducing yourself with
A little bit of charm.
The last time I checked, being a
Gentleman didn't do any harm.
But once again I apologize that your game
Was not compatible with your looks.
But hopefully the next girl will
Consider adding your number to her phone book.

Never Say Never

There are so many things
I said that I would never do,
But for the sake of time
I'll only name a few.
Looking back on the past
Smiling and thinking, if I only knew
That thoughts and views
Don't stay the same,
And as your mind gets wiser
Your perspectives begin to change.
The same things it seemed that
I was boycotting
Are now the things I'm standing
Up like an advocate, shouting.
I had a list of characteristics
Stipulating the men I'd date
But as I got older that
List was overpowered by fate.
I never imagined you
You contrasted so many things on my list
But, because you were for the better
And not the worse,
I was willing to take that risk.
You brought to the table
Qualities that could not be defined on paper.
I was attracted to your exceptionally,
Unique character.
I never could have imagined your distinct features
That looked so good up against mine.
Or how in-depth your personality would be
And how quickly our spirits would intertwine.
I never thought I could love someone
More than my first love
Then after being with you, I realized
That I never really knew what it meant to be loved.
So ironically, I threw out the list that
Defined my ideal man

For I was baffled that
My soul mate (you) did not fit into that plan.

Question

Winding and twirling in a world of confusion—where the only thing certain
is that I'm uncertain of who I am.
Being drugged by the poisons of the world's perceptions,
Insecurities and glam,
I become dependent on the opinions of others.
Clothed in a pseudo image with an altered Personality; my image begins to
Blend in with my surroundings.
While on the inside my true inner being
Is drowning.
I am now a classified depiction of what "they" consider normal;
Whereas my formal image was looked upon as being informal.
So I stop and ask the question **Who am I**?
Could I be a hopeless soul in a hopeless body,
Trapped by make-up, perms, and the latest trends?
Could I be in a socially excepted warfare that I don't think
My soul is going to win?
I've become a combination of many looks, from those idolized on television
To those admired in fashion magazines.
I'm a stirred up mixture of a laid back look, to diva style
And everything else in between.
There is no unique distinction about myself.
I'm caught up in a world where the acceptance of my appearance is
dependent by my wealth.
There is no room for creative differences or individuality,
For most of us are bound by an extreme makeover mentality.
Conformed in an era the states "if my clothes are fine and my hair is tight,
Then I must be all right.
If the tag on my shirt is somewhat recognizable,
Then my look is more than likely expectable.
So again I ask the question, **Who am I**?
I'm first of all a person admitting to be confused.
Confused that this image of myself might actually even be me,
But I have to stop and question the motivation of the image
And maybe that answer will set me free.
So here I stand before you, completely naked and all exposed.
Stripped of my insecurities that clothed me from my head to my toes.
Attempting to back track unto those days were I had my own identification.

Where my style was not lumped into a group or specific classification
And being myself was simply okay and I did not have to change my
appearance to match the world's fashions that changed from day to day.
I stand bare before you questioning who I am
Questioning the power of influence
Questioning one's inner self—verses one's outer
I question the rationale of our thinking and of our actions
The spiritual verses the physical
But most of all, I question will you QUESTION!
Who you are and whose you are!

Concluding Stages

Hurt, pain and confusion
Is what I feel.
I can't sleep on it or wait around,
Cause even time won't heal.
Just when I let my guard down,
And let him in
Fates takes place and I feel I can't win.
I'm so scared to act on impulse for
I have to rationalize,
I'm not ready to continue and that I realize.
But when faced in the assertion seat
My feelings start to play tricks
And the words my mouth will
Speak, I'm scared to predict.
I've sat still, so many times and began to cry,
Then I realized, that the future
Can't wipe my eye
For I'm not in denial about this guy.
I'm conscious of all possible outcomes,
But I'm scared to view the end.
That is why I know deep down inside
A serious relationship should not begin.

Broken

Two hearts once united
A relationship now undecided
Feeling the need to belong
And that feeling now too strong.
I'm trying to reopen the door to your heart
While you're turning the key with intentions to lock.
My heart longs to be reunited with you
For it answers to no one else's knock.
"Give love another chance," I say
And make it stronger each and everyday.
Don't just throw away the key
Pick it back up again, for I need you to see
That nowhere has my love gone
And without you I'll spend my whole life alone.
Please send your love again
So that my broken heart can mend
All the pain it's been through
And release this sadness which has left me feeling blue.
I'm asking, if our two hearts can be united again?
Or is this how it ends, with me just being a friend.

Magical

Last night you kissed me and
It was a kiss so soft and sweet.
And even though I did not tell you,
I felt as if I floated off my feet.
We both got caught up in a moment of impulse
In which I never wanted to end.
With each touch of your lips
A part of me melted within.
And like the wind blows, who knows
In which direction this will lead us,
So I allowed myself to live in the moment
And I accepted that time as glorious.
As the world faded into darkness
The two of us began to illuminate
Nothing else mattered at that time
Except for you, me, and fate.
Who ever said that dreams don't come true,
Wasn't there the night when I was kissed by you.

If It's Okay?

I want to love you
And that's kind of hard for me to say.
I want to be your girl, your wife
And one and only lady.
I want to be in your world and not in your way.
I want to make it possible for you
To be with me and not feel the need to stray.
Allow me to be apart of your life,
Giving you love and affection
Without all the strife.
Give me a chance to comfort you
After a long, hard, tiresome day.
I guarantee, I'll do it in the
Most satisfying way.
Allow me to be your black
Cup of coffee in the morning
And your final glass of fine wine
That leaves you longing
For my Folgers the next time you arise.
Let me stare deep into your eyes
So that we can see each other's soul
While allowing our inner secrets to unfold.
Permit me to be that key to your heart
That's been locked up for so many years.
Let me unlock the jammed door
To all of your deepest fears.
Allow me to help you grow
Into the man God wants you to be.
Encouraging your ambitions
To let you reach your highest destiny.
Allow me to be that strong woman
Who will stand by your side
Because being with you
Is where I want my heart to reside.

Nothing but the Best

The qualities I'm looking for in a man
Are nothing but the best.
But of course he must be
God fearing and nothing less.
See when I talk about my man
You have to understand
He must be a brother and no other color.
He has to be a tall drink of water
To quench the thirst of my father's daughter.
He must be truthful and all that I want
For when I speak, I want to be blunt.
Therefore, he must be deep
And profoundly on my level
For the words I spit,
He should not have to dig for with a shovel.
His personality must be off the chain!
For it is not real intriguing to kick it with a lame.
I want to be able to sit around and act a fool
Hanging out breaking about every rule.
When it comes to a conversation,
I should not want it to ever end
That is just how good our vocal skills must blend.
Now on to the topic of looks;
He must be at least fair.
I know all are beautiful to God
But attraction must be there.
I would get started on hair:
Braids, fades, dreads and all,
But to be honest, it would not even
Matter if my man came bald.
As long as he knows how to work well
With what he got
That means being himself instead of
Someone he's not.
One who knows how to treat a lady
The way a lady is suppose to be treated.
That means the rules of chivalry, he can repeat it.
If into my life he cannot deposit

A relationship with me won't even get started.
I need a man who meets my qualifications
Cause I'm not out there looking
For cheap thrills, nor donations.
I need a man who will step up to the plate
Do the right thing and take me on a real date.
Someone who knows how to appreciate
Lu for what she has to offer,
So if you're not that man, don't even bother.
Cause the qualities I'm looking for in
A man, are nothing but the best,
And again I say, he must be God fearing
And nothing less.

Holding On

I'm holding on because I love him.
Even though he doesn't show it
I know he loves me too.
See we've been through so much together
And I feel confident that things will get better.
He's all that I got.
I've even tried to move on, but I just cannot.
His face is embedded in my brain
And even in silence I hear echoes of his name.
I've invested all of my energy into his life
And I'm hoping that things will change
Once I become his wife.
So I'm holding on because I know that
He will eventually change his ways
And him saying, "I won't hit you again"
Will be a past tense phrase.
And that as my bruises heal
So will my heart
And our relationship will be
Like it was from the start.
His hits of anger and frustration
Will become strokes of love
And we will rekindle the romance
In which I'm still dreaming of.
Maybe I see what others can't see, or maybe I see
The potential in which he could be.
I love him so much, so much
That I don't know why
I would deny myself the freedom to fly
Away from this bondage of love and pain
A love that lacks pride but promotes shame.
I'm in a catch 22, for I'm afraid to leave
Yet I'm even more afraid to stay
So my mind escapes to the false
Realities of a better day.

The Boy Next Door

Remember how back in the day, we could just
Chill out playing with us and our imaginations.
Though now it seems that our thoughts of each Other are filled with
infatuation.
Reminisce back to the days where we could talk
On the phone about almost any and everything.
But now we are scared to converse for
We are uncertain of what the next conversation Might bring.
See before puberty, we were tight.
We had freedom without expectation
Which made everything alright.
But as I've gotten older
The boy next door has become the man
That my heart longs for
Now I don't know what to do with
This state of confusion I have fallen in.
I want to gain you as a companion
But I don't want to loose you as a friend.
I've always known you as the one I
Could depend on and the one I could talk to.
No matter how serious my situation, you would
Always be there to see me through.
And if I were to loose that
I don't know what I would do.
What happens if it doesn't work out
Or if I continuously walk around
With this feeling of doubt?
What if we discover it was curiosity
Instead of love,
In which our relationship was all about?
I'm trying to play it cool, but I'm so nervous and you can tell
For I don't want to be another one of those girls
Who got caught up in a temporary spell.
I want to know that it's real
And I want a guarantee
Before I jump into this pool of mystery.

Running Back

Dear God, if America is the land of opportunity,
I must be a prisoner in my own community.
I'm locked away from all the good stuff,
Trying to get off on good behavior
But my actions aren't enough.
After receiving two degrees,
I'm greeted with a recession.
I'm trying to smile and tell you I'm fine,
But I'm really battling depression.
Staying with family ain't easy,
Believe me, I know these things.
I know why the cage bird sings.
It sings because when it was finally let go,
It had to make a u-turn and return
When the money and jobs didn't flow.
I'm like a college student before they get
Their refund check—broke.
Broke like paying bills after Christmas and
It isn't a joke.
I have to make hard life decisions
Weeks before payday,
Like, do I eat, put gas in my car,
Or pay Sallie-Mae.
When is my piece of the pie
Going to get sliced?
When am I going to roll a seven on my dice?
Lord you said that you would give
Me the desires of my heart,
But lately it seems that you've only placed disappointment in my cart.
It seems like the closer I get to accomplishing
My goals,
The further away it seems for me to
Cross over the threshold.
I know my name isn't Wall Street,
But I too need a bailout.
I've been traveling down this dead-end road
For too long and I need a new route.

My momma never said it was going to
Be days like this,
So I assumed that after college,
Life was going to be bliss.
Instead, it seems that I have one flag,
While everyone else has six.
I have more bills than money, which is like having oil and water—
They just don't mix.
I can't get a good job without experience
And I can't get experience without a job.
And if one more company tells me they're just accepting applications,
I'm going to sob.
I'm going to shed a tear for every bill I don't have enough money to pay.
For every time a friend asked me to go out and I had to tell them,
"Maybe another day."
For the times when my hair has been jacked up
And a ponytail was all I could do.
For the times I looked at the clothes in my closet and convinced myself
That old was the new, new.
I'm tired of struggling to reach this seemingly,
Unobtainable, American dream.
A dream that really means, it's not what you know, but who you know that's
going to get you the cream.
So God, since you are the CEO of the world,
I need you to make a position for your child.
Create me a job that will make all of my struggling seem worthwhile.
I know my treasures aren't to be stored here on earth,
But can I at least get one gold nugget to justify my birth.
I'm trying to be patient, but my patience is wearing thin.
I'm trying to be content and not claim defeat,
But sometimes it seems I just can't win.
God, if you are listing, please help me out
And tell me what you want me to do.
I've tried it my way and failed,
So now, God, I am running back to You.

<u>When Life happens to you, what will you do?</u>
<u>Will you call on God to pick you back up on your feet,</u>
<u>Or will you fall back and retreat?</u>

~ Romans 3: 23-24 ~
"23 for all have sinned and fall short of the glory of God, 24 and all are justified freely by his grace through the redemption that came by Christ Jesus."

<u>Call on God!</u>